From Heaven Above

The Story of Christmas
Proclaimed by the Angels

PATRICIA *and* FREDRICK McKISSACK

Illustrated by BARBARA KNUTSON

Augsburg

To Mavis, Bob, River, and Amy

FROM HEAVEN ABOVE
The Story of Christmas Proclaimed by the Angels

Copyright © 1992 Augsburg Fortress

Scripture quotations unless otherwise noted are from the Holy Bible: New International Version. Copyright © 1978 by the New York International Bible Society. Used by permission of Zondervan Bible Publishers.

ISBN 0-8066-2609-7   LCCN 92-70385

Manufactured in the U.S.A.   AF 9-2609

96   95   94   93   92   1   2   3   4   5   6   7   8   9   10

1

"Then an angel of the Lord appeared to him, standing at the right side of the altar of incense. When Zechariah saw him, he was startled and was gripped with fear. But the angel said to him: 'Do not be afraid, Zechariah, your prayer has been heard. Your wife Elizabeth will bear you a son, and you are to give him the name John. He will be a joy and a delight to you, and many will rejoice because of his birth.'"

Luke 1:11-14

Shelby didn't know what to think! Grandpa had been acting strangely all morning. She had followed him up the stairs and down again—in one room and out another—searching for something, looking, looking everywhere.

She watched with wide, wondering eyes as Grandpa climbed up the steep attic steps to that dark, shadowy place where scary thoughts lived. She remembered the time the attic door had stuck shut behind her, and she shivered with fear. She didn't follow Grandpa there. But he didn't seem to notice.

Shelby started to put her thumb in her mouth, but then clutched Clyde, her stuffed camel, instead. "Grandpa?" she called up the steps. "Are you all right?"

Of course he wasn't all right, Shelby decided. She hoped he'd be better by evening. They were going to decorate the Christmas tree.

Thump! Bump! Shelby could hear her grandfather dragging heavy boxes and pushing and pulling old furniture around. What was he looking for?

"Grandpa!" Shelby called out again. "What are you doing?"

The noises stopped suddenly. Silence. Shelby listened to the quiet. "Do you think Grandpa's heart attacked him like Grammy's did?" she asked Clyde. The button-eyed camel said nothing.

What if Grandpa was sick? What if he needed her? Shelby had to go up to the attic to see. So, tucking Clyde under her arm, she tip-toed up the steps, hoping that by being very quiet she wouldn't disturb the scary things that waited in the dark.

She peeked inside the attic room. A circle of light filtered through a small, round window. Grandpa was kneeling beside the old cedar chest, looking at things—old things.

"Grandpa," Shelby whispered. "I know how to call 911 if you need me to."

Grandpa looked up, smiling. "Come," he said, beckoning for her to join him.

Fear locked Shelby's legs. "I'm scared," she said, squeezing Clyde closer and wanting very much to suck her thumb.

"I understand," said Grandpa. "I really do understand."

Then, with slow and careful hands, he unfolded a package wrapped in crinkly tissue paper. Inside was a beautiful lace angel. "I finally remembered where Grammy put this. She crocheted this angel for you. It was the last thing she made." He held up the angel in the circle of light. "She said it was the first Christmas angel."

Shelby took one small step into the room. At the same time, Grandpa began a story: "God sent an angel to tell Zechariah that his wife Elizabeth was going to have a son. They were to name him John."

"I know what happened," Shelby said, taking another step and another. "Zechariah didn't believe the angel. He thought he and Elizabeth were too old. Because he didn't believe, he couldn't talk until the baby was born."

One more step.

"And when Zechariah could talk again," Grandpa continued, "he said John would prepare the way for the light from heaven that would shine on people living in darkness."

"I know who that light was," Shelby quickly added. "Jesus!"

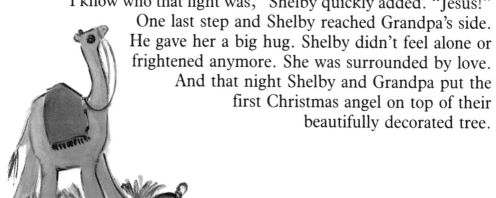

One last step and Shelby reached Grandpa's side. He gave her a big hug. Shelby didn't feel alone or frightened anymore. She was surrounded by love.

And that night Shelby and Grandpa put the first Christmas angel on top of their beautifully decorated tree.

2

"But the angel said to her, 'Do not be afraid, Mary, you have found favor with God. You will be with child and give birth to a son, and you are to give him the name Jesus.'

" 'I am the Lord's servant," Mary answered. 'May it be to me as you have said.' Then the angel left her."

Luke 1:30-31, 38

Daniel had been helping out at his grandfather's jewelry cart at the mall during the holiday season. It was lunchtime, and Grandfather had left Daniel in charge for the first time. He wanted to do his best.

A steady stream of shoppers had been stopping by to look at the fine pieces of silver and turquoise jewelry, sometimes buying, but more often just admiring the quality craftsmanship.

"No wonder this piece is so beautiful," said one shopper, examining a ring closer. "See the *DM?* Those are the initials of David Mangas. He's a master craftsman—the best! I'll take this," she said, handing the ring to the boy.

Daniel beamed with pride. He wanted to tell the woman, *My grandfather is David Mangas*, but he knew Grandfather didn't approve of anything that came close to bragging.

Meanwhile, another shopper had stopped to browse. Daniel saw her looking at the small silver angel he thought he'd hidden behind some larger pieces. Quickly, Daniel showed the shopper a pair of earrings marked down to half price. The customer grew annoyed and moved on without buying anything. Daniel felt terrible.

But he couldn't help wanting the angel. He had wanted it since the day Grandfather had fashioned it from a scrap of silver. It was small compared to Grandfather's other pieces—not much bigger than his thumbnail—but designed simply and beautifully.

While Grandfather had worked on the piece, he had told Daniel a story. "Angels are God's messengers," Grandfather had said. "God sent the angel Gabriel to tell Mary she was going to have a baby. It must have been frightening for Mary, but she trusted God."

Daniel loved the story and the small angel he called Gabriel. Secretly, he wanted it, but he knew that wasn't possible. Grandfather earned his living with his jewelry, and his pieces were very expensive.

Then along came an opportunity. Grandfather had asked Daniel to work for him during the holidays. "For payment," he had said, "you may choose a piece from whatever is left, as a gift for your mother." Daniel had his heart set on the angel. He didn't want anyone to buy it.

When Grandfather returned from lunch, he praised Daniel for doing a good job of managing the cart. But Daniel didn't feel so praise-worthy. What if he knew I had cost him a sale? he worried.

The day dragged on. Shoppers came. Some bought large, expensive pieces. Very few even looked at the shiny silver angel. Daniel felt guilty. He moved the little angel up front. Maybe someone would see it and buy it. Then he wouldn't feel so awful.

Near closing time, a man stopped by. "I have one gift left to get. Just something small. Let me see that little angel you've got there."

"I can give you a better deal on this pair of earrings," Grandfather said, steering the man away from the small angel. "Half price. In fact, I'll even take off an extra twenty percent since it's so late in the day and tomorrow is Christmas."

Grandfather chuckled softly as the man left with his purchase. "Closing time! And we finally got rid of those earrings." Then, winking his eye, he said, "Just as I promised, you can choose any piece left as your payment."

"I want Gabriel," Daniel said with a broad smile. "We'll put it on our tree. Mother will love it, especially when I tell her the great story you told me."

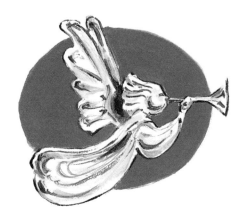

3

"An angel of the Lord appeared to him in a dream and said, 'Joseph son of David, do not be afraid to take Mary as your wife, because what is conceived in her is from the Holy Spirit. She will give birth to a son, and you are to give him the name Jesus, because he will save his people from their sins.' "

Matthew 1:20-21

Asa was almost six, but he couldn't ever remember seeing either one of his grandfathers in person. Mama's father had passed away before Asa was born, and Dad's father was a Navy officer who was always in some faraway place. But Asa's sister Liza and brother Jason talked about their grandfather all the time.

Asa had seen pictures of Big Dad, and he had talked to him on the phone. Dad had told him stories of Big Dad and the ship he commanded. Now that he was a rear admiral, he was going to live and work in Washington, D.C. There was a long article in the paper about his promotion, and he had had his picture taken with the president. Now he was coming to celebrate Christmas with Asa's family.

What if he doesn't like me? Asa worried. What if he thinks I'm stupid? When Asa saw the big man standing in the front hall, all his imaginings became real. I know he's going to hate me!

"Come to Big Dad," the man said, holding out loving arms. Liza and Jason bounded toward him, but Asa held back, clinging to his mother's leg for security.

"Go on," Mama coaxed.

Asa didn't move. He looked wild-eyed and frightened. Suddenly Big Dad spotted him. He smiled and stooped down to speak. "You don't remember me, do you," he said. "Last time I saw you, you were two years old. What are you now? Five?"

"Almost six," he answered shyly. Asa allowed Big Dad to hug him, but he quickly wiggled loose.

Big Dad turned to hug Mama and Daddy and all the other relatives who had come for the holiday. The house was noisy and full of wonderful smells. Mama had been cooking Virginia ham, sweet potato casserole, cookies, pies, and plenty of eggnog.

After dinner, Big Dad told stories about his ship, his new job, and all the places he had been. Liza sat in his lap, and Jason was draped across the arm of his chair. There was no room for Asa, so he sat on the floor by the fireplace. Of course he likes Liza and Jason better—they're bigger, he told himself.

Suddenly Big Dad left the room. When he returned, he gave Mama a small box. "I want you to open this now, even though it's not Christmas yet." Inside was a beautiful glass angel. "I thought it would look great on your tree," Big Dad said, smiling. Daddy agreed. Mama passed the angel around for everyone to see.

When the angel reached Asa, it slipped from his hands and fell on the marble hearth, breaking into many pieces. "I'm sorry. Honest. I didn't mean to drop it!" Asa said, batting tears away. "Now I know you'll hate me! I don't care!" And he rushed from the room.

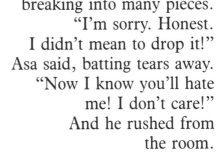

A few minutes later, someone knocked on his bedroom door. "Go away!" he cried. But the door opened and in walked Big Dad!

"Okay! Up off the bed!" he ordered. "There's work to do." He spread out the shattered angel on Asa's desk, and set down a bottle of glue. "We have to put this angel back together."

For the rest of the evening, Asa and Big Dad worked on the angel. They talked about lots of things, about making mistakes, about being afraid, and about loving and caring.

Then Big Dad told a story: "This broken angel reminds me of Joseph, after he heard that Mary was going to have a baby. He was all broken up inside. He loved Mary, but he wasn't sure he should marry her. But God sent an angel to tell Joseph that Mary's baby was God's Son."

"Joseph felt better then, right?"

"Yep," said Big Dad. "You know the rest of the story. Mary's baby, Jesus, came to help all the broken people in the world—including you and me."

At last they finished. Together they took the angel downstairs and put it on the tree. The lights glittered through the cracks, making the little glass angel sparkle like crystal.

4

"An angel of the Lord appeared to them, and the glory of the Lord shone around them, and they were terrified. But the angel said to them, 'Do not be afraid. I bring you good news of a great joy that will be for all the people. Today in the town of David a Savior has been born to you; he is Christ the Lord.' "

Luke 2:9-11

Maggie was happy about the neighborhood association Christmas party, but she was even happier that Grandpop had come from the mainland to spend Christmas with them. He was going to the party, too.

"Come on, Mom," Maggie called impatiently, "or we'll be late!"

"Okay! Okay!" Mom said in her no nonsense voice. "We'll get there. We'll get there."

Grandpop smiled at Maggie, his eyes twinkling merrily. Maggie clapped her hands. They were on their way to the party—at last.

The decorating committee had decked the beach pavilion with garlands of Hawaii's most beautiful flowers, and as each person arrived, they were presented a lei. Torch lights, soft music, and gentle sea breezes combined with the smell of roasted pig and other goodies to make this Hawaiian-style Christmas feast a very special gathering.

Everything looked wonderful; everything tasted even better. But Maggie could see that something was troubling Mom. "What's wrong?" she whispered.

"I'm in charge of the entertainment, and I've just learned that the band I hired cancelled at the last minute. I don't know what to do."

Maggie scanned the pavilion. "Lots of people here would be willing to help out," she suggested. "Why don't you ask a few if they would perform."

"I suppose I could. . . ." her mother mused.

Maggie looked over at her grandfather. He was surrounded by a group of people. He seemed to be having the time of his life, doing what he did best—telling stories. An idea popped into Maggie's head. She hurried over to Grandpop and whispered something into his ear. He gave his approval with a brisk nod, and Maggie rushed back to Mom. "The party isn't over yet," she said with a wink.

A little while later, the impromptu program began. Willie Dey played a medley of Christmas carols on the guitar. Tommy Obe recited a poem, and his sister Ann danced the story of the first Hawaiian Christmas.

Then Maggie got up to introduce a special guest: "Straight from the Napa Valley in northern California, I present to you the best storyteller in the world, my Grandpop, Mr. J. D. Koramatsu."

Grandpop bowed graciously as he took the stage. "There is no story more beautiful than the birth of our Savior, Jesus," he said, and as Grandpop began his story, he also began folding a piece of paper.

"When Mary and Joseph reached Bethlehem, there wasn't room for them at the inn. So they found shelter in a stable."

Grandpop folded the paper over and over. "And that is where the Christ child was born. And his mother wrapped him in swaddling cloths and placed him in a manger."

Grandpop held up the folded paper. Without using scissors, paste, or tape, he had made a beautiful paper angel.

Everyone clapped with surprise. Mom looked relieved. She sent Maggie her own special wink.

Then Grandpop explained that he'd used the ancient Japanese art form of origami—paper folding—to make the angel. He showed everyone how to use their paper placemats to fold their own origami angels.

"An angel of the Lord appeared to the shepherds outside Bethlehem," Grandpop continued. "The angel told the shepherds that the Savior had been born. Then a multitude of angels appeared, all singing praises to God."

When they got home, Grandpop and Maggie put their angels on the Christmas tree. "This is the best Christmas ever," Maggie said, yawning. And she fell asleep, listening to Grandpop tell yet another wonderful story.

5

"An angel of the Lord appeared to Joseph in a dream. 'Get up,' he said, 'take the child and his mother and escape to Egypt. Stay there until I tell you, for Herod is going to search for the child to kill him.'"

Matthew 2:13

LaShonda's grandfather taught history at the university. He pulled into the faculty parking lot and shut off the motor of the car. There were no classes during Christmas break, but he still stopped by his office every few days to check the mail and messages.

"You can wait in the car or come up," Papa Sam said. "We'll go shopping afterward."

LaShonda answered by bounding out of the front seat and rushing ahead of him, kicking a path through the snow. She wouldn't dream of missing a chance to visit Papa Sam's office.

His office always felt much smaller than it was because of the clutter. Every corner was occupied by a file cabinet, table, or bookcase, and they were usually filled with books, papers, and folders.

Ma Jo said Papa Sam would dry up like a leaf if he stayed away from his books and papers for more than a day or two. LaShonda believed it, too. She couldn't imagine not having books.

While Papa Sam looked through his mail, LaShonda studied the books on his shelf. There was a new biography about Frederick Douglass, the great abolitionist. The words were too hard for her to read right now, but she had her own book about Frederick Douglass that she could read. He was one of her favorite heroes. She loved reading about the slave's flight to freedom. But Douglass's story left LaShonda feeling very angry about slavery. How could people be so mean?

Papa Sam was making a few telephone calls, but LaShonda didn't mind. Her curious eyes moved around the office, taking in decades of her grandfather's work. That's when she saw the small wooden angel, half-hidden by the appointment calendar and pencil holder. It was highly polished and gracefully carved. She'd never seen it before. Where had it come from?

"I'd love to hear more about that proposal at the beginning of the year," Papa Sam said, ending his telephone conversation. Returning the receiver to its cradle, he noticed that LaShonda was admiring the angel.

"So you discovered it," he said, pushing back in his chair. "It's an unusual piece. It resembles many of the sixteenth-century wood carvings from the Congo. It might have come to this country aboard a slave ship. But, oddly enough, it was found here in Ohio."

LaShonda studied the angel with excited fingers, letting the smooth wood tell her its own story.

Papa Sam continued. "When they tore down the old Chandler Building they found a room beneath the main basement. They discovered all kinds of articles down there—like this mahogany angel. Seems it was a station on the Underground Railroad."

"Just like in the story of Frederick Douglass? That's how he got away. Heavy stuff."

"The founder of this university was a conductor on the Underground Railroad. He helped hundreds of slaves escape."

LaShonda turned the angel over in her hands. "Just think, some captured African held onto this angel through the awful journey into slavery. And then maybe some runaway slave girl—a lot like me—held on to it to keep her from being scared during the dangerous journey to freedom."

"Possible." Papa Sam put his coat on, and helped LaShonda with hers. "Sometimes slaves used Bible stories to help understand their own situations," he explained. "So this angel might have reminded someone of how an angel came to Joseph in a dream and told him to take Mary and Jesus to Egypt because Herod wanted to kill the baby. The slaves were running for their lives, too."

Papa Sam gave LaShonda the angel. "You may keep it," he said, hugging her. "I hope it always reminds you of how much I love you, and also that God's love protects us both."

"I'll put it on the tree tonight!"

They stepped out into the cold afternoon. A dull sun hid behind light gray snow clouds. LaShonda touched the little angel in her pocket and felt warm all over.

6

"After Herod died, an angel of the Lord appeared in a dream to Joseph in Egypt and said, 'Get up, take the child and his mother and go to the land of Israel, for those who were trying to take the child's life are dead.' "

Matthew 2:19-20

Pops was an ex-truck driver turned cook. He and his grandson Mikey ran a diner out on I-35, named POPS. Pops was all the family Mikey had. But Pops was a great family.

As long as Mikey could remember, at Christmastime Pops had decorated the diner and the house out back with thousands of glittering lights, twinklers, blinkers, chasers, and bubblers. The place looked like it was on fire. Then there was the Christmas tree, filled with hundreds of ornaments, each one with its own story.

This year, Mikey had been feeling lonely. Christmas was family time. But Pops was his whole family. Sometimes Mikey longed for brothers, sisters, aunts, uncles.

On the night before Christmas, just before closing time, a couple with three children came into the diner. Mikey grumbled under his breath. It had been a long, hard day and it was time to go home. But Pops never turned away a customer. Besides, these travellers looked like they needed help.

"Come on in. Have a seat," Pops said, moving from behind the counter, menus in hand.

"No." The man shook his head. "No food. I'm Tomas Mendez. This is my wife Gloria and our three daughters. Our car broke down. We saw your lights and came here to get help. We are trying to get home for Christmas."

"You came to the right place," Pops said, placing the telephone on the counter. "There's a station about a quarter of a mile north of here. You can get a tow into Laredo. But it might take a while."

Twice Tomas Mendez refused food, but Pops wouldn't take no for an answer. "Can't brag about *ambiance*," he joked, "but the place is clean, the coffee is hot, and the food is . . . well two out of three ain't so bad."

That made them laugh. They relaxed, and Pops busied himself making big, juicy hamburgers for everybody, including Mikey and himself. They all ate homestyle like a big family, and afterward, Pops told stories about his Christmas tree ornaments.

Mikey knew the stories, too. "See the star on top? It's the star of Bethlehem," he told the girls. "It led the wise men to Jesus. And they came bringing gifts of gold, frankincense, and myrrh."

By that time the tow truck arrived, and it was time for the Mendez family to be on their way again. Pops refused to take any money for the meal. "It's my Christmas gift," he said.

As Mikey was cleaning off the table, he found a small straw angel by the napkin holder. "Pops, look what they left."

His grandfather smiled widely. "Another story for our tree." He placed it in a prominent place.

"What story will you tell about the little straw angel?"

Pops thought for a moment. "Hey, I've got a perfect one. You know, there were lots of Christmas angels—more than Gabriel and the heavenly host. This story is about the *last* Christmas angel. The one who came to Joseph in Egypt. You see, an angel came to Joseph in a dream to tell him it was okay to take Mary and Jesus back home to Nazareth."

Mikey hung up the dish towel. "The Mendez family was trying to get home, too. I wonder if someone helped Mary and Joseph and Jesus on their trip home."

"I don't know," Pops said, shutting off the light. "But, let's call it a day and go home, Michael."

Mikey looked back at the big Christmas tree, shimmering in the darkness. "Pops, what do you get when you take a mother, father, brother, sister, and grandmother and mix them all together?"

"I don't know, what?"

"One big, loving grandfather—the best family a guy could have."

And Pops's laughter resounded through the night air.

"Suddenly a great company of the heavenly host appeared with the angel, praising God and saying, 'Glory to God in the highest, and on earth peace to men on whom his favor rests.' "

Luke 2:13-14